drawing close

Other books by Graham Cooke

Crafted Prayer
Developing Your Prophetic Gifting
A Divine Confrontation
God Revealed
The Language of Love
The Secret of a Powerful Inner Life
When the Lights Go Out

drawing close

See God's Face and Be Changed Forever

being with God series

Graham Cooke

Chosen
Grand Rapids, Michigan

Published by Chosen Books
A division of Baker Publishing Group
P.O. Box 6287, Grand Rapids, MI 49516-6287
www.chosenbooks.com

Originally published under the title *Beholding and Becoming* by
Sovereign World Limited of Tonbridge, Kent, England

Printed in the United States of America

Library of Congress Cataloging-in-Publication Data is on file at
the Library of Congress, Washington, D.C.

ISBN 0-8007-9385-4

I dedicate this journal to the members of Odyssey, the businessmen's spirituality group in California that I co-lead with my great friend Tim Dickerson.

Our times together have been a compelling mixture of grace, the search for truth, impacting dialogue, friendship, laughter and good wine. Thanks!

contents

Acknowledgments   9

Introduction   11

Drawing Close   15
    Mary, Not Martha   15
    Revival Shows Our Weakness   16
    Living Water   18
    Be Renewed   19
    God's Kind of Warfare   20
    What the Church Can Be   23
    Real Church, Real Worship   27
    Find Your Peace   32
    Testing Your Peace   36
    Spreading Your Peace   42
    What Rest Looks Like   43
    Quiet Times   44
    Bouncing Back   46
    Finding Joy   48

Rejoicing Every Day   51

Untouchable Joy   52

Laughter on the Battlefield   56

The Promised Land   60

Contrition and Joy   62

Not Enough Laughter   63

Acquainted with Grief   66

Thriving in Life   68

Conclusion   71

Exercise 1: Lamentation   74

Exercise 2: A Promise from Ephesians 3:14–21   81

Exercise 3: *Lectio Divina*   85

FAQs (Frequently Asked Questions)   91

About the Author   93

acknowledgments

I want to thank the journal team of Carole Shiers (my personal assistant), Tim Pettingale (my friend and publisher) and his staff at Sovereign World, and Jordan and Jenny Bateman (editorial). They are a great bunch to work with on a project so close to my heart. Their tireless work, enthusiasm and unflagging good humor have helped to make this project one of life's great pleasures.

Together, we are all *Drawing Close*.

introduction

You carry a profound and unfathomable call on your
life, placed there by God Himself. It is fresh and new
and completely beyond your natural ability to
accomplish—God has called you to do something you
cannot possibly do. You can meditate on that call for
the rest of your days, strategize it to no end, even try
and seize it; it doesn't matter. Like reaching for the
stars, God's call is beyond you. It's a gift God has given
each one of His children. In fact, your inability to
accomplish it is exactly why He has selected you to
carry that call.

    As rational human beings, faced with a world bound
by goals and measures, we find this difficult to believe.
But the apostle Paul didn't: "God has chosen the
foolish things of the world to put to shame the wise,
and God has chosen the weak things of the world to
put to shame the things which are mighty," he said in
1 Corinthians 1:27. We are the "foolish" and the
"weak" to whom Paul referred—we cannot think our
way into fulfilling the call of God. Fortunately, He has
not asked us to. God has that covered; His most foolish

moment is greater than our wisest and grandest revelation. Paul explained that, too: "Human wisdom is so tinny, so impotent, next to the seeming absurdity of God. Human strength can't begin to compete with God's 'weakness'" (1 Corinthians 1:25, Message). If we cannot grab hold of this great call, what can we do?

As Christians, we must learn to live in the consistent nature of God. The Father will never change His heart toward us. Like the father in the story of the Prodigal Son (see Luke 15:11–32), He only wants to love His children, no matter their decisions, mistakes or successes. When we live in that place of consistency, we get to walk with God into the unpredictable and outrageous. Our lives become an adventure, full of laughter, courage and miracles. In the Bible, saints who walked in consistency got to walk on water, see an ax head float, witness the sun standing still in the heavens, raise a child from the dead and part a river's water. They were pushed by God to a place where even creation obeyed them.

> "It's kind of fun to do the impossible."
> Walt Disney

Creation longs for that breakthrough again. "For the earnest expectation of the creation eagerly waits for the revealing of the sons of God," Paul wrote in Romans 8:19. The landscape of the Western world—in the United States, United Kingdom, Canada, Australia and all points in between—is waiting for a different Christian to emerge from the cozy confines of the

Church. A different type of believer is needed. The ground itself longs to see the sons of God rise up, a tribe with the power of the Holy Spirit indwelling their lives. To them, the experience of the miraculous is largely irrelevant; those mighty works don't matter nearly as much as the One making them possible. Don't walk away from the personhood of God; too many people in the renewal movement of the latter half of the twentieth century did just that. Do the absurd thing—enjoy the experience you're having, but adore the One who is giving it above all else.

We must learn to behold the glory and intimacy of God and become like Him. We need to come into a place of rest where everything that God is can come and touch us. We must stop striving and simply *be*. To fulfill our call, we must be Mary, sitting and waiting at the feet of Jesus, not Martha, running around behind the scenes.

drawing close

Mary, not Martha

The story of Mary and Martha is familiar to many of us. Let's look at it, once again, in Luke 10:38–42:

> Now it happened as they went that He entered a certain village; and a certain woman named Martha welcomed Him into her house. And she had a sister called Mary, who also sat at Jesus' feet and heard His word. But Martha was distracted with much serving, and she approached Him and said, "Lord, do You not care that my sister has left me to serve alone? Therefore tell her to help me."
>
> And Jesus answered and said to her, "Martha, Martha, you are worried and troubled about many things. But one thing is needed, and Mary has chosen that good part, which will not be taken away from her."

In our Western thinking, we prize activity more than anything else. We feel we always have to be doing

something—waking up, walking the dog, driving the
kids, teaching Sunday school, picking up the kids,
cooking dinner, cutting the lawn, waxing the car and
on and on and on. We are a whirlwind of activity,
just like Martha, getting ourselves worked up over
everything. Mary, meanwhile, seems lazy to us. Where
is the measurable fruit from her day? What has she
contributed? Why won't she help her sister serve this
important houseguest? Mary's conduct is foreign to our
thinking.

Yet it is Mary whom Jesus commends; her rest has
served her well. Mary was being consistent in her
relationship with Jesus. The biggest desire in God's
heart is inhabitation. If you search through the
Scriptures, you'll find that coming and living with His
children is all He has ever wanted. What we usually
pray for, however, is another move of God.

revival shows our weakness

Unlike inhabitation, there is no call for revival found
anywhere in Scripture. The Church, quite simply,
should never need reviving. Revival is not about
getting people saved; revival is about the Church
coming back to her original purpose before God. I
think it's very sad that so many of us have prayed
and longed for revival—it means the Church is a long
way from what God wants us to be. Maybe, just

maybe, a little touch from God could bring us immediately into line. That's the mystery of life with the Godhead—you just never know what could turn the tide of history.

We see this in our own lives quite often. One day we're yearning for something, and the next day that thing is fulfilled. How on earth did that happen? What swung the hinge so quickly? It was simply Jesus, coming to inhabit something. This is one of the deep things of God, one of those spiritual mysteries that is hidden, waiting to be revealed. The gospel writers recorded that Jesus did not trust what was in the hearts of men; my prayer is that God would trust us enough to show us—and do—something new.

> "I believe that the imperative need of the day is not simply revival, but a radical reformation that will go to the root of our moral and spiritual maladies and deal with causes rather than with consequences, with the disease rather than the symptoms."
> A.W. Tozer

For me, revival can be defined as the Church coming back to a place where God can trust us with the things He really wants to give us. When that happens, there will be a reformation, a move of God in which the walls of the Church will be knocked flat, and what we have in the meeting is what we have in the marketplace. Miracles will happen, God will be in full evidence, people will get saved by the hundreds of thousands and creation's longing for the sons of God to move in power will be answered.

living water

To experience this move of God, we must let Jesus inhabit us. We must drink of His living water, as He described in John 7:37–38: "On the last day, that great day of the feast, Jesus stood and cried out, saying, 'If anyone thirsts, let him come to Me and drink. He who believes in Me, as the Scripture has said, out of his heart will flow rivers of living water.'" If we are thirsty to fulfill the impossible call of God, we need to drink in Christ's love, allowing Him to fully inhabit our lives.

Water is an allegory Jesus used several times in His ministry to explain His effect on the earth. In John 4, He met a woman at a well, and told her, "If you knew the gift of God, and who it is who says to you, 'Give Me a drink,' you would have asked Him, and He would have given you living water" (John 4:10). He later added that "whoever drinks of the water that I shall give him will never thirst. But the water that I shall give him will become in him a fountain of water springing up into everlasting life" (John 4:14). Inhabitation fulfills us at the deepest level, dividing what is our soul—our mind, will and emotions—from our spirit—our conscience and ability to commune with God. Jesus, whom the apostle John also referred to as the Word of God, splits our spiritual

> "When we remain in the Spirit, we abide in Christ, and Christ has the ground to abide in us to carry out His divine dispensing in us."
> Watchman Nee

being from our soulish behavior. "For the word of God is living and powerful, and sharper than any two-edged sword, piercing even to the division of soul and spirit, and of joints and marrow, and is a discerner of the thoughts and intents of the heart," the author of Hebrews wrote in chapter 4 verse 12. We must learn how to keep these two things apart, and how to teach our soul to be a vehicle to the movement of our spirit.

be renewed

This process is called being renewed. "Therefore we do not lose heart. Even though our outward man is perishing, yet the inward man is being renewed day by day," Paul wrote (2 Corinthians 4:16). We have been saved, we are being saved, we will be saved. Salvation is one thing; conversion is another. Many Christians just stop with salvation, but we are called to be converted into the image of Jesus. Salvation without conversion isn't going to get us anywhere, because life is a journey. We need to learn how to be transformed and conformed to the nature of God. Life is not about coming to Christ; it's about becoming Christlike.

> Life is not about coming to Christ; it's about becoming Christlike.

If God lives in you, you are in the presence of God. What a starting point! God is in me, and I am in the presence of God. God is in you, and you are in the presence of God. We can live that way. When you come into a quiet time, relax—you're in God's presence. Allow the Holy Spirit to develop your patience when it comes to your quiet times. Let Him discipline that part of your nature, conforming it to the example we have in Jesus, a Man who would spend forty days fasting, who would pray all night and who would wait on His Father. Patience and peace are difficult sometimes, but remember Paul's words: "I can do all things through Christ who strengthens me" (Philippians 4:13). Devotion is about being, not about doing. It's about being Mary, not Martha. There's no place to which we must rush; we're already there. God is in us, and we are in the presence of God.

Striving to get to that place will do us no good—we already live there. So enjoy it! Embrace the enfolding love of God Himself. He is the Alpha and the Omega, the Beginning and the End and everything in between.

God's kind of warfare

Because God's presence is always with us, He is the answer to the spiritual warfare we face. The peace of having Him overshadow our lives gives us a powerful weapon. Many times in Israel's history, God told the people to do unconventional things: sing, march,

The Caim—An Ancient Celtic Prayer

Christ be with me,
Christ within me,
Christ behind me,
Christ before me,
Christ beside me,
Christ to win me,
Christ to comfort and restore me,
Christ beneath me,
Christ above me,
Christ in quiet,
Christ in danger,
Christ in hearts of all that love me,
Christ in mouth of friend and stranger.

shout, wait. *You don't need to fight,* He whispered to them, *because this isn't about you; it's about Me. I'm not asking you to strive and pull down things. I'm asking you to make room for Me to act.*

"The LORD is a man of war; The LORD is His name," the Scriptures tell us (Exodus 15:3). We serve a warrior king, and one of the best places to be with Him is on a battlefield, outnumbered by the enemy and hearing Him laugh in their face. *Is that all you've got?* He chuckles. Hearing the joy of the battle and the heart of God is utterly incredible. Spiritual warfare is about discovering the majesty of Jesus and the sovereignty of God. It's about an oak tree growing out of the root of our relationship with God—strong, steadfast, powerful, massive.

> "My defense is of God, who saves the upright in heart."
> Psalm 7:10

Our goal as a church must be to facilitate, with the help of the Holy Spirit, the presence of God among us. Church isn't about meetings; it's about worship, making God an offering and prayer. Everything we do in church must be God-centered. This is temple worship, and God is restoring it to His people.

The Holy Spirit wants to do two things with us: First, He intends to get us to a place where we trust God *for* everything, and *with* everything; and second, He seeks to bring us to a place where *He* can trust *us*. The Father will always trust what He sees manifested of the Son in our lives ... the inhabitation of Jesus. It's a pleasure to trust God, knowing that His great love will catch us, even if we fall off the edge of a cliff. This great God will send us out into battle against impossible odds with a seemingly ludicrous battle plan. *March around the enemy for seven days and then shout,* He'll say, winking at you the whole time. "Go your way; behold, I send you out as lambs among wolves," He says (Luke 10:3). Fortunately, you're a lamb with a Lion as a friend.

God does not send His children out weak and defenseless, but as soldiers who are vulnerable to who He is. When you're truly vulnerable to God, the Lion can walk with the lamb. No enemy will come against you. "No weapon formed against you shall prosper," as was prophesied in Isaiah 54:17. I am completely convinced that there is a place in God where we can confuse and exhaust the enemy. We can confound him, making him tear his hair out with frustration because his attacks only make us stronger in spirit. If he ignores us, we'll rip him apart. If he attacks, the Lion will devour him. This is the place in the Spirit to which God is trying to take us.

what the church can be

In 2 Corinthians 3:7–18, we get a taste of what Paul thought the Church could be:

But if the ministry of death, written and engraved on
stones, was glorious, so that the children of Israel could
not look steadily at the face of Moses because of the
glory of his countenance, which glory was passing
away, how will the ministry of the Spirit not be more
glorious? For if the ministry of condemnation had
glory, the ministry of righteousness exceeds much more
in glory. For even what was made glorious had no glory
in this respect, because of the glory that excels. For if
what is passing away was glorious, what remains is
much more glorious.

Therefore, since we have such hope, we use great
boldness of speech—unlike Moses, who put a veil over
his face so that the children of Israel could not look
steadily at the end of what was passing away. But
their minds were blinded. For until this day the same
veil remains unlifted in the reading of the Old
Testament, because the veil is taken away in Christ.
But even to this day, when Moses is read, a veil lies on
their heart. Nevertheless when one turns to the Lord,
the veil is taken away. Now the Lord is the Spirit; and
where the Spirit of the Lord is, there is liberty. But we
all, with unveiled face, beholding as in a mirror the
glory of the Lord, are being transformed into the same
image from glory to glory, just as by the Spirit of the
Lord.

Let's not settle for something as small as what we
have defined to be "revival" when there is a larger
blessing to be had. We do not have to be like Moses,

who put a veil over his face so that his friends and countrymen would not look intently at what was fading away. To this day, when the Mosaic Law is read, a spiritual veil separates God from man. This veil, Paul teaches, can only be removed by a love for Jesus Christ. Whenever a person turns to the Lord, the veil is ripped to shreds. "Where the Spirit of the Lord is, there is liberty," Paul wrote. "But we all, with unveiled face, beholding as in a mirror the glory of the Lord, are being transformed into the same image from glory to glory, just as by the Spirit of the Lord."

We must keep our eyes focused firmly on the cross. Christians who are only intent on pulling down the strongholds of the enemy have not seen the fuller picture. If they had, they would be instead intent on pulling down the very glory of God into their midst. Satan is not the focus of the Church; the Bridegroom is. The only answer to darkness is to switch the light on, and become so full of Jesus that He fights for us. The glory of God, living in God's presence, and being full of His light must be our preoccupation. We are not seekers of the enemy; we are seekers of God. When God comes to us in power, the enemy comes looking for us! And when he does find us, the enemy comes face-to-face with the One who is with us. A stronghold is pulled down when our intimacy with the Lord intimidates the enemy.

> "A lifestyle of intimacy intimidates the enemy."

With increased passion comes an upgrade in favor. Intimacy, passion, presence and favor all lead us into a greater experience of the glory of God.

Many churches are faced with the same problem as Moses, in that the glory of God is rapidly fading from their face. They are in a season of transition in which successes are dwindling—but a new glory of God is about to emerge. What will define the Church in the next season is not the usual hallmarks of attendance, facility, budget, equipment, mission work or even five-fold giftings. These things have only a partial impact on the work of a church. What will define success in this next time period is the amount of the glory of God that is resting upon His people corporately. As people become intent on one thing—God's glory—only attracting Him to our midst will be important.

I don't just want to believe *for* God's presence; I want to believe *in* God's presence. I want to see it, taste it, hear it, smell it and feel it. I want meetings in which, without anyone doing anything, no one can stay standing. I have been privileged to be in meetings where rain has fallen inside the building. Where the power of God is so thick that you worship for hours, and the last sound you hear is an exhausted drummer falling through his kit. I've been in meetings where oil has covered everyone's foreheads. Where people have been healed even though no one prayed for them. Where lights have appeared and danced around the room. Meetings where hundreds of people heard the voice of God, and no one spoke. Where money appeared in people's pockets, and no one knew how it got there. Poor people walking out of a service wealthy.

I've had many tastes of God's glory—now I want it to become commonplace. The unity and the glory Paul described can happen in our churches: "Now the Lord is the Spirit; and where the Spirit of the Lord is, there is liberty. But we all, with unveiled face, beholding as in a mirror the glory of the Lord, are being transformed into the same image from glory to glory, just as by the Spirit of the Lord." It can happen.

real church, real worship

I cannot overemphasize the importance of returning to temple worship. The Jews of Jesus' time had two different types of worship in which to engage. In the synagogue, they could hear the word, receive ministry and have fellowship. In the temple, worship was about interacting with the presence of God. I think we need both forms of worship in our churches, but perhaps not at the same time. My favorite meetings are the ones where we "waste" a lot of time on God. Two, three, four hours, perhaps stretching into the early hours of morning, just worshiping and magnifying God's name: I love that.

To worship is to enter the presence of God.
Worship is vital to our spiritual health; that's why
you must have a personal plan to
worship this year. I encourage you to
consider how you want to grow in
personal worship. Ask yourself: *What's
going to change? What's my strategy
going to be? What time am I going to
allow? What am I going to do this year that I didn't do
last year?* A vision without a plan is just wishful
thinking.

> "The instinct to worship is hardly less strong than the instinct to eat."
> Dorothy Thompson

Worship is a multifaceted thing; there are many
different frequencies. *Lamentation,* for example, is the
most powerful form of worship, but we rarely talk
about it. God loves lamentation because it is the only
form of worship that we can do in the absolute reality
of where we are. We cannot hide anything in
lamentation, and God doesn't ask us to. In our lives,
there are times when our situation is inescapable.
A loved one dies; our grief is powerful and absolute.
We cannot put our issue and feelings aside.

Lamentation is when we step into the very thing that
is bothering us and worship God anyway. It is stepping
into our pain, stepping into the reality of what life is
like for us. "Though He slay me, yet will I trust Him,"
Job said (Job 13:15). *Here I am, Lord,* a lamenting
worshiper says. *Things are bad, but You are glorious,
and I worship You.*

Habakkuk, an Old Testament prophet, understood lamentation well:

> Though the fig tree may not blossom,
> Nor fruit be on the vines;
> Though the labor of the olive may fail,
> And the fields yield no food;
> Though the flock may be cut off from the fold,
> And there be no herd in the stalls—
> Yet I will rejoice in the LORD,
> I will joy in the God of my salvation.
>
> Habakkuk 3:17–18

Things can be grim, but God is the same. He is as worthy of worship on our worst day as He is on our best. Lamentation worship is about two words: *though* and *yet*. *Though* the trees are not blossoming and the fields are not producing, *yet* I will rejoice in You. Lamentation is a cold-blooded act of will—pushing our emotions aside and choosing to worship. God, knowing the trust it takes to lament, has an indescribable and indefinable way of coming and being with us when we worship in our most painful moments. It is the most sincere form of adoration that exists, and God loves it and inhabits it.

> "It is in the process of being worshipped that God communicates His presence to men."
> C. S. Lewis

In worship, we must live in the "yet," not the "though." The heart of a decent relationship with God is to never mind the "though" because there is always the "yet." Though the world crumbles, yet will I worship You. Lamentation isn't about worshiping God to try and trick Him into blessing us; it's about saying, *All of these things are true, but I don't care—I still want to worship You. I'm not going to ask for anything; I'm just going to worship.*

At times, we can't help but live in the "though." Difficult things happen, and we struggle to worship. But in the life of a Christian, there is always the "yet." Trust in the "yet." Sing about God's majesty, that though you feel pain, yet you will adore Him. Set your heart to worship no matter your circumstance, no matter the style of worship.

Thanksgiving enables us to enter into His presence. The truth is that God is always with us, whether we feel Him or not. He is perpetually present. Our emotions are a wonderful bonus, but we live by faith. If we give thanks for His presence in all things, our anticipation will release expectation. It's cool to be thankful.

We *praise* God for who He is. We call up His names and thereby rejoice in His nature. He becomes our focus of appreciation and value. We look to Him and our faces are lightened.

In *adoration*, we express our total delight and confidence in God. Our role in the earth is to be occupied with Jesus. We need to be too busy being fascinated with Him to be intimidated by the enemy.

There is a romance, a language of love, a rest in the storm that only comes out of our value to the Father. Adoration flows out of joyful acceptance. *High praise* is an adventure. In His presence, we get to reverse the events that consume us by having our attitude and perception joyfully adjusted. In the adversity of life, we can put everything on hold when we deliberately give ourselves to the excitement of involvement with the Holy Spirit in praise.

It is a wonderfully provocative and deeply spiritual experience to deliberately turn your back on a problem in order to face God in exaltation. Lift your eyes and exult in Him. The situation may not have changed, but you have become different. What we behold, we become.

Warfare praise is the coolest thing to do when the enemy is present and working. One can stand in front of the enemy and revel in the majesty of God. Warfare is about lifting your eyes above the foe and seeing God, present and happy. It is calling to the One who is more than a conqueror; it brings down His names and exults His sovereignty.

At times, the battleground seems to disappear for me, and I am enveloped in the cloud and fragrance of God's glory. Time passes, and when the cloud dissipates, so has the enemy.

God is unveiling our faces and removing anything that keeps us from focusing on Him. He is letting us into a holy place we've never seen or experienced before. Worship is for life, not just for meetings. You can only give corporately what you are giving individually.

When we discipline ourselves to behold Jesus in every circumstance, a transformation occurs. We learn how to sit, wait and watch for Him every day. The Holy Spirit teaches us about face-to-face, personal adoration; it comes from a worship that flows from a place of rest. When we sit at Jesus' feet and just be, as Mary did, we behold Him. Worship cannot come out of striving, but out of stillness. Spending time with God gives us a touch from Him—this touch is such a pleasure that it will cause a spirit of adoration to well up in us, and overflow. Jesus isn't looking for Mary to reach up to Him and try to curry favor; He is looking for Mary simply to be with Him, allowing Him to reach down and honor her.

find your peace

Mary knew how to be still. She knew where her peace could be found. In the bustle of her sister's work, Mary knew that to truly enjoy Jesus, she had to step back and simply *be*. One of the fruits of the Spirit listed in Galatians 5:22–23 is self-control. Self-control, in fact, is the only form of control acceptable in church life. Practice taking your thoughts captive, and you'll soon find that they won't wander away from God's promises, even on your worst and most potentially anxious days. "And do not be conformed to this world, but be transformed by the renewing of your mind, that you may prove what is that good and acceptable and perfect will of God," Paul wrote (Romans 12:2). It is part of the Holy Spirit's job to help us transform our minds. Ask Him for help, and He will do just that. He loves the process of bringing us to a place where we live in the "good and acceptable and perfect will of God."

When our mind is fixed on God, our heart is fixed on Him. There should be nowhere to go to in your devotional life because you're already there. Enjoy the discipline of being at rest. Devotion should be different from prayer—don't mix the two. Sometimes when we come into our quiet time, we have too much of an agenda: "Pray for this, pray for that, thank You very much." We need to just sit and adore Him, experiencing who He is. "Inspire me, Holy Spirit," should be our whisper. When we sit and worship Him, the Holy Spirit can then move on us and lead us to pray about the people and situations He wants to see changed. We shift from our task list of prayer to His.

> "Worship is giving God the best that He has given you. Take time to meditate before God and offer the blessing back to Him in a deliberate act of worship."
> Oswald Chambers

Throughout the day, how many times do you step back and worship God? Take time, even five minutes, simply to worship. It can make a world of difference.

Years ago, I worked for a training company. Often, I would go into my office and ask my secretary to hold my calls for ten minutes. I'd close the door, sit down at my desk and spend ten minutes adoring Jesus. On really rough days, I'd make it twenty minutes.

On one particularly rotten morning, I was finishing a twenty-minute session. I came out of my office to let my secretary know that I was ready to face calls when I heard her tell someone on the phone, "Oh, you can't disturb him right now, he's worshiping." And she wasn't a Christian! I looked at her, shocked.

"What did you say?" I asked.

"I told them you were worshiping," she replied.

"How did you know?"

"I figured it out," she said. "I know you're a Christian, and I know that you go into that office stressed and come out totally different."

I took her out for lunch, and we talked more about it. I was amazed at what she had picked up, just from observing me. "You went in stressed; you came out peaceful," she told me. "I realized you and God have been getting along in there."

Don't come with things to do until you go into the business of prayer. When it comes to real devotion, come with nothing to do except to sit and learn how to wait, rest and be. Be still. Fill your mind with Jesus. Faith and stillness are sustenance for your spirit, so learn to focus on Jesus. When your mind wanders off topic, bring it back. Retrain it; it's had years of having its own way. Renewing your spirit and your mind is exciting and has incredible fruit. Worship becomes natural for you, and the peace of God wells up in your heart. God's perspective can be seen more quickly. The helmet of salvation, which Paul mentioned in Ephesians 6:10–20, is the rest of God, protecting your thought life. Take some time out to discipline your soul in peace and rest.

Psalm 46 tells of worship that starts with an earthquake:

> Therefore we will not fear,
> Even though the earth be removed,
> And though the mountains be carried into the
> midst of the sea;
> Though its waters roar and be troubled,
> Though the mountains shake with its swelling.
>
> Psalm 46:2–3

The psalmist disciplines himself to hear God's voice in the midst of all the shaking, and the song ends with a new revelation of God:

> "Be still, and know that I am God;
> I will be exalted among the nations,
> I will be exalted in the earth!"
>
> Psalm 46:10

Stillness is a critical part of growing up in the Spirit
and truly knowing the presence of God. When the
landscape shifts beneath your feet, be
still and know He is God.

"We only learn to behave
ourselves in the
presence of God."
C. S. Lewis

Immature, or soulish, Christians
come into a shaky situation praying,
If it be Your will, Lord. The Spirit-led
Christian, however, prays, *Father, I ask
You to do this.* There's a world of difference in the faith
levels of those two prayers. A soulish Christian will
pray in hope; a spirit Christian will pray in faith. There
is a certainty of God's presence.

testing your peace

Our circumstances are not the house in which we are
called to live spiritually. The name of the Lord is our
strong tower and refuge, and we have to discipline
ourselves to live there, and not in our issues. Mary ran
to the feet of Jesus while Martha lived in the kitchen.
If you're enjoying your life at the moment, learn to be
happy in the happiness of God. There is a place in
God's heart for you. If you're in a time of grief, then
let God come and comfort you. Either way, God wants
to come to you in what is happening. He may come as
your Comforter, wrapping His arms around you and
holding you tight, even as you cry into His chest. He
may come as your Prince of Peace, calming your

emotions. He may come as your King of Joy, laughing and swinging you around. Just come to God as you are.

We live by grace. Good days and bad days don't exist; there are only days of grace. Some days, the grace of God allows you to enjoy life, and other days, endure life. Don't think about good or bad—just think about grace. *I have grace for this, to enjoy it and to have a really good time,* or, *I have grace for this, to endure it.* Find Mary's heart, learning to come, to sit, to be, to wait, to rest, to abide in Jesus. Waiting for God is our age's great discipline. "But those who wait on the LORD shall renew their strength; they shall mount up with wings like eagles, they shall run and not be weary, they shall walk and not faint"—this is the promise from Isaiah 40:31 for us.

Why are so many Christians stressed out, tired, anxious, burned out and living with a negative emotional lifestyle? It is our lack of ability to rest and our inability to live in "day-tight" compartments. We allow yesterday's issues to spill over into the next day. "New every morning" is the promise of God's compassion and lovingkindness. Just as the Israelites were given new manna every morning in the desert, God's mercy is always fresh.

Our experience of God becomes stale when we do not treat each day as new in His presence. What new things may occur if we lived in the newness of life

A Prophetic Word

Cross over, My children,
From all you have known, seen and tasted of My presence.

For all that has passed before you on the journey of worship
Has been to bring you to this place.

For I am taking the heart of stone
Out of the lives of My people
To free them from selfish restraint and self-preoccupation
That they may behold Me.

In these days, I will be your reward as you worship.
You will enter into that place of adoration
That the angels occupy around My throne.

For it shall be on earth, even as it is in heaven.
Worship from the earth shall ascend and meet
Worship descending from heaven.
When the first heaven meets the third heaven
In adoration,
All that is demonic in the second heaven
Shall be displaced by the weight of glory.

For I shall come down into that place of adoration
As you seat Me on the throne of your passion.
When I come, all things will change.
I will adorn My bride with My beauty
And make her ready for My intimate embrace.

Cross over, My children,
Set your heart to cross over
Into a new land of worship.

Press in, press in,
Learn to stand in joy and admiration.
Receive the stamina, the discipline, the will
To push your heart forward.

Give yourself, do not withhold,
But push, push on, push through.
Give birth to a new song
That will captivate your heart as it captivates Mine.

This song will fill the earth.
It will fill My house.
It will fill My temple
Even as it fills your heart.

A new land awaits you.
Go in and possess your possessions.

In worship, in adoration,
Receive My longing for you.
Let My aching heart refresh you,
Replenish you, restore you.

promised to us in Scripture? In Romans 5:1–5, we see the life in Christ that we have been given:

> Therefore, having been justified by faith, we have peace with God through our Lord Jesus Christ, through whom also we have access by faith into this grace in which we stand, and rejoice in hope of the glory of God. And not only that, but we also glory in tribulations, knowing that tribulation produces perseverance; and perseverance, character; and character, hope. Now hope does not disappoint, because the love of God has been poured out in our hearts by the Holy Spirit who was given to us.

The apostle Paul knew this concept well. "The life which I now live in the flesh I live by faith in the Son of God, who loved me and gave Himself for me," he wrote in Galatians 2:20. Paul learned how to live from the inside to the outside. He never doubted that God loved him or was with him. He never wondered if God was listening or if He was speaking. We must follow Paul's example in this.

> "We are so often caught up in our activities that we tend to worship our work, work at our play, and play at our worship."
> Charles Swindoll

God will test your commitment to rest, peace and adoration. He used the wind and waves to test His disciples, for example, in Mark 4:35–41:

On the same day, when evening had come, He said to them, "Let us cross over to the other side." Now when they had left the multitude, they took Him along in the boat as He was. And other little boats were also with Him. And a great windstorm arose, and the waves beat into the boat, so that it was already filling. But He was in the stern, asleep on a pillow. And they awoke Him and said to Him, "Teacher, do You not care that we are perishing?"

Then He arose and rebuked the wind, and said to the sea, "Peace, be still!" And the wind ceased and there was a great calm. But He said to them, "Why are you so fearful? How is it that you have no faith?"

And they feared exceedingly, and said to one another, "Who can this be, that even the wind and the sea obey Him!"

Jesus knew the storm was brewing, and He decided to seize the moment to gauge His disciples' faith. *We'll take the boys for a boat ride and see what they're made of,* He thought to Himself. As the waves began to roll, Scripture tells us Jesus was sleeping. I sometimes wonder if maybe He just had His eyes closed and was praying: *Make the waves really big, Father. Let's see what Peter and the lads have in them!*

As the storm raged, the disciples panicked. Some of them were experienced fishermen who had sailed all their lives—things must have been bad for them to get that scared. As they rowed and cowered and hung on

for dear life, they looked to the back of the boat. There
was their friend Jesus asleep. *How can He rest at a
time like this?* they thought. *How can you* not *rest at
a time like this?* Jesus thought back.

When a storm is howling, it's a perfect time to rest.
Practice the presence of God at all times when the
storms come against you; you'll realize that it's a
perfect opportunity to establish that peace even more.
When you rest in God, the wind and the waves cannot
touch you. They cannot move you; they cannot hurt
you. Resting in God means we are being powered by
the internal presence of the Almighty, not the external
storm.

spreading your peace

Out of His own rest, Jesus spoke the words the disciples
had longed to hear: "Peace, be still!" That's our job on
the earth, to spread the peace God has given us. Every
newspaper we read, every television program we
watch, is consumed with conflict. Wall-to-wall
coverage of war, disaster and scandal—in a word,
conflict. Where are the peacemakers in the midst of it
all? Where are the Christians who know how to live at
peace in the storm? To where have we vanished? Out
of His peace, Jesus spoke peace.

"Blessed are the peacemakers," Jesus preached in
Matthew 5:9, "for they shall be called sons of God."

There have been times when I have walked into a room and the level of peace and faith has risen. When things are hard and we call extraordinary prayer meetings, I know that I can come, carry my devotion to rest and see peace grow. Why? It's a simple principle: What you take in with you comes out and is distributed. If you enter a room with bitterness, bitterness is what you distribute. If you enter a room with peace, peace is what is given away. Whatever is in you comes out. If you're operating soulishly, then you will detract from what God wants to do; if you're acting in a right spirit, you'll add to what He is doing.

what rest looks like

Rest is a better way to live, but it can cause misconceptions. You can live in such a place of rest that people will accuse you of not caring. It's as if they think that someone can't care unless he or she is all worked up. But an anxious, fearful person is less likely to get an answer from God than one who is living in rest. God is always close by; "I will not leave you nor forsake you," He promised in Joshua 1:5.

> Jesus said, "Come to Me, all you who labor and are heavy laden, and I will give you rest."
> Matthew 11:28

God likes to hide—in fact, He invented the game Hide and Seek. In certain seasons, He will reveal Himself to us; in others, He will hide from us. God only hides because He wants to teach us to look for Him. We all want Him to be manifest in our lives, all the time, but God sometimes wants to hide and draw us deeper into His presence.

If God is hiding from us—but He has also promised never to leave nor forsake us—we can extrapolate one thing: God is hiding in plain sight, teaching us to look for Him in a different way. God is unpredictable but completely consistent. We always know where we are with God because He never changes, but we seldom know what He's going to do next.

God will push us into places where we are not equipped to be. To survive and flourish there, we have but one choice: Seek God in a place of rest. Let Him carry us forward. God hasn't called us to do the reasonable, the possible or the attainable. He has called us to do the outrageously impossible.

quiet times

Quiet times are about to be touched by God in a new and powerful way. We need this shock to our system of doing things; we have been so enslaved by our evangelical mindset that we have tried everything, except rest, to reach out and grasp God. But the true discipline of the spirit is to learn how to be touched by Him—how to sit at His feet, as Mary did, and be loved for simply *being.* If you knew how much God wants to touch you, wants to speak to you, wants to be with you, you would never doubt Him again. If you knew the intensity of God's heart for you, your life would be changed.

The Holy Spirit has many duties and responsibilities, but one of His great pleasures is teaching us how to abide in God. He loves to discipline us in staying, dwelling and remaining in Him. Transformation takes place when we rest in His everlasting arms. So wait joyfully, knowing that God is about to change you forever.

To have an effective devotional life, we must understand the difference between the soul and the spirit. In Scripture, the soul—our mind, will and emotions—represents the striving of man to achieve something or be successful at something. The spirit, however, represents God's place of rest and peace within us. "Abide in Me, and I in you. As the branch cannot bear fruit of itself, unless it abides in the vine, neither can you, unless you abide in Me," Jesus said in John 15:4-5. "I am the vine, you are the branches. He who abides in Me, and I in him, bears much fruit; for without Me you can do nothing."

> "Bidden or not bidden,
> God is present."
> Erasmus

Learning how to abide in the power of Jesus is the great challenge facing the Church today. We must learn to live from within, knowing that God isn't out there in space somewhere, but inside us. Praying for the Holy Spirit to come is irrelevant—the Holy Spirit is already here. A Spirit-led man or woman recognizes God's presence and thanks Him for being with him or her. *Teach me how to wait, to be still, to live by faith,* a Spirit-led Christian prays. *You said You would never leave us nor forsake us, and I know it to be true. Thank You. How can I serve You?*

bouncing back

A call has gone out from heaven to the Church: Learn how to turn and yield within yourself to the presence of God. This is a discipline we need to practice every day of our lives. It may not come easily, but we must not be discouraged—God is in the beginning, and He will also be there in the end. It doesn't matter where you are or what you feel; God is with you, and that's enough. Be faithful and withdraw your heart from outward distractions. Turn away from them, and yield to God on the inside. Forget Martha's dishes in the sink, and sit at His feet like Mary did. Form a habit of turning inwardly to God and abiding within Him.

Turning and yielding to God refreshes us. We learn how to bounce back when we fail. One of my early mentors watched me grow frustrated as I kept falling into temptation—I was very hard on myself. "Do you know what the best way is to harass the enemy?" he asked me one day.

"Tell me," I said.

"Bounce back from a defeat as quickly as you can," he answered. "Perfect the art of bouncing back, and one day, there will be nothing to bounce back from."

Nothing is more disconcerting for the enemy than seeing you bounce back from a defeat into which he took so much time to lure you. The blood of Jesus cleanses all sin—when you bounce back in repentance, it tears down all the work of the enemy. Sometimes intimacy with God is blocked by the rubbish within ourselves; if we can change our mind, however, the Holy Spirit will change our emotions. Intimacy with God is about allowing the love of God to come in and displace the rubbish that is present.

God has planted a divine "Yes" in your heart. "For all the promises of God in Him are Yes, and in Him Amen, to the glory of God through us," the Bible says in 2 Corinthians 1:20. Your heart wants to be in that "Yes" place with God.

At the end of the day, it is the loveliness of God that is going to accomplish the promises in your life. Through His goodness, His kindness, His peace and His joy, He will strengthen you. Learn how to sit and rest and wait and be. Fill your mind with Jesus, and your life will never be the same.

finding joy

Along with stillness, joy is a key to the principle of beholding and becoming like Christ. In Psalm 27:4, we see how much David longed to behold the face of God—"One thing I have desired of the LORD, that will I seek: That I may dwell in the house of the LORD all the days of my life, to behold the beauty of the LORD, and to inquire in His temple." Like David, we must be people who cannot wait until heaven to see the beauty of God—we desire it now. We can have eternal, abundant life here on earth. Anything that happens in heaven can happen here, now. And I believe that joy is an important piece of beholding God's face now.

One of my favorite verses is 1 Peter 3:9, which talks about the blessing we are called to inherit. There is an inheritance and favor over your life right now. God has a stream of continuous blessing for you that He wants to release—if you are not presently living in it, you are robbing yourself of incredible joy. We are called to inherit this blessing for ourselves, and for everyone around us. What if the promise of God in your life was so large that it could cover ten square blocks in your community? Wouldn't you want to know what that blessing is? God is extravagant and lavish enough to do that—and much more.

> "Laughter is part of the human survival kit."
> David Nathan

Being glad in the Lord is an essential element in
salvation. Salvation restores our capacity for joy,
gladness and laughter. "You will show me the path
of life; in Your presence is fullness of joy; at Your
right hand are pleasures forevermore," David wrote
(Psalm 16:11). The angels understand this concept—
they were the ones who got to deliver the Good
News first. Throughout the gospel of Luke, we sense
their joy and excitement over the news they
announced:

► "Do not be afraid, Zacharias, for your prayer is
   heard; and your wife Elizabeth will bear you a
   son, and you shall call his name John. And you
   will have joy and gladness, and many will rejoice
   at his birth" (Luke 1:13–14).
► "I am Gabriel, who stands in the presence of God,
   and was sent to speak to you and bring you these
   glad tidings" (Luke 1:19).
► "Rejoice, highly favored one, the Lord is with you;
   blessed are you among women!" (Luke 1:28).
► "Do not be afraid, for behold, I bring you good
   tidings of great joy which will be to all people.
   For there is born to you this day in the city of
   David a Savior, who is Christ the Lord" (Luke
   2:10–11).
► "Glory to God in the highest, and on earth peace,
   goodwill toward men!" (Luke 2:14).

"Good tidings of great joy." Is there a clearer, more profound description of the emotion we are to experience when we ponder the message Christ brought? Our evangelical impulse should be to share the fact that there is a joy that can infect and change every person on the face of the earth. It can touch every single inhabitant of this planet. The joy of God is so immense that when it is released, it can touch billions of people at the same time. Everything that God touches turns to laughter and rejoicing.

> "At the height of laughter, the universe is flung into a kaleidoscope of new possibilities."
> Jean Houston

When God shows up, creation laughs. This idea was captured beautifully in Psalm 96:11–13:

> Let the heavens rejoice, and let the earth be glad;
> Let the sea roar, and all its fullness;
> Let the field be joyful, and all that is in it.
> Then all the trees of the woods will rejoice before the
>   LORD.
> For He is coming, for He is coming to judge the earth.
> He shall judge the world with righteousness,
> And the peoples with His truth.

God is a happy God. In fact, He is the happiest Person I have ever met. Every day, we can say, "This is the day the LORD has made; we will rejoice and be glad in it" (Psalm 118:24). Every day of our life with Him should be marked by laughter, joy and rejoicing, because that's the only thing we can be when we come face to face with how supremely happy God is. He even sings over us with joy—that's how happy God is.

rejoicing every day

To be joyful takes an act of our will. We must choose to rejoice every day. Twice, the apostle Paul gave us that advice: "Rejoice in the Lord always. Again I will say, rejoice!" he wrote (Philippians 4:4). He was even clearer in 1 Thessalonians 5:16: "Rejoice always." Paul knew God intimately and had come face to face

> "Laughter is the shortest distance between two people."
> Victor Borge

with His sunny disposition. He had learned that laughing and rejoicing opened people's hearts to the reality of who God is.

Learning how to live in Christ makes us vulnerable to laughter. Laughter is more than a choice; it's a requirement for us that we be happy. God's highest plan for our lives includes a desire for us to find, live in and love the joy that is in Christ. God is good news! His love and presence is an absolute tonic for us.

"These things I have spoken to you, that My joy may remain in you, and that your joy may be full," Jesus said (John 15:11). Every time God speaks to us, or reveals more of His nature to us, joy is part of that equation. Beholding Him and becoming like Him is an invitation to party and celebrate with Him. Everything God says to us is designed to bring us into joy. Everything in the Kingdom of heaven is about gladness, joy, happiness and laughter. God is joyful news, and He wants to bring a smile to our faces.

untouchable joy

God is joyful because He knows what is coming next. He knows the final score. When you know the end from the beginning, you can't help but laugh at all of the enemy's schemes and tricks. They become irrelevant when you know that you win. There is a continuous joy in Christ that runs so deep that no one else can even touch it. But to access it, we need to learn how to rejoice in all things.

For me, joy is a safeguard. It's a shield against the enemy. While rest is a weapon, joy is a shield behind which we can hide. When the enemy comes, we can laugh in his face—because God laughs at him first.

I once had a dream where I was on a battlefield. We had just fought off the enemy, but we had lost a lot of good people. There weren't many of us left; we were small and pitiful, to be honest. Every one of us was wounded. I myself had at least a dozen sword gashes on my arms. I was bleeding badly and was absolutely exhausted.

Suddenly, a trumpet blew, and I saw another enemy army take the field in front of us. I looked around but saw no reinforcements for our battered side. The enemy was powering up. Their ranks were swelling with every passing moment. It was a hopeless fight, but our ragtag band of survivors gathered close together and got ready.

As I set my feet and gritted my teeth in preparation for the enemy's charge, I noticed that a man next to me was dressed as a restaurant waiter, with perfectly pressed black trousers; a bow tie; a crisp, white shirt; and a white towel slung over his arm.

"What are you doing?" I asked incredulously.

"Would you like the melon or the soup?" he replied.

"What?" I asked.

"Melon or soup?" he said.

"How can you talk about food at a time like this?" I demanded.

The waiter ignored me and went from person to person, asking, "Melon or soup?"

"Are you mad?" I said. "Don't you see what's happening? Don't you see the blood all over the ground? Don't you see the enemy over there? How can you talk about lunch at a time like this?"

"Mmm-hmm," he answered. "Melon or soup?"

I lost my temper completely. "Are you stupid or something?" I screamed. "You want to talk about food at a time like this?"

Suddenly, I woke up to find myself shouting, "Talk about food!" in my bedroom. In that instant, I received a powerful revelation, found in Psalm 23:5: "You prepare a table before me in the presence of my enemies."

When we're on the battlefield just trying to survive the next wave of the enemy, God is thinking about menus. He looks around and says, "What a great place for a picnic! We can have sausage rolls, meat pies, cheese sandwiches. This will be perfect." I fully understand that this is a bizarre way of thinking, but then so is the thought that God is not extremely happy, full of joy and laughter. Why are so many people attracted to Jesus? It's because He is not solemn or miserable. At the end of their all-too-brief sojourn on earth, good servants are told, "Well done; enter into the joy of the Lord." Confident people are always happy. Jesus is so secure in who He is and in His power to defeat any enemy that He can feed us in the middle of the worst battle of our lives.

> "Laughter is an instant vacation."
> Milton Berle

I had a second dream that illustrated the same idea. Again, I was on a battlefield, but this time the armies hadn't fought yet. Again, my side was completely outnumbered. The enemy was huge in stature—the soldier in front of me was eighteen feet tall. I was getting a headache just looking up at him! The enemy was salivating at the prospect of crushing us. They had better weapons, greater numbers and were bigger, stronger and faster.

It was another hopeless battle. I decided that even though I was going to die that day, I wanted to take a few of these guys out with me.

As I mustered up the nerve necessary to charge the enemy line, I had the impression that I should look up. I looked at the enemy soldier in front of me, starting with his boots, and then all the way up to his head. Imagine my surprise when I saw Jesus grinning and waving just a couple of feet above the bad guy!

"Psst," Jesus whispered. "They don't know I'm here." I looked deep into His eyes and saw the joy He was feeling. One person with God is always in the majority.

"This is going to be so cool," Jesus whispered happily. "Look into his eyes now."

I looked the enemy straight in the eye and saw a fear that hadn't been there before. He was terrified of me, because the way I looked had changed. I was full of faith, confidence and joy in my Savior. When I beheld Jesus, I became like Him—and that worried the enemy. When we look into the eyes of God and hear Him laughing, something changes in our persona.

God laughs at His enemies. When we're in a fight, He looks at the enemy and says, "Hey, is that all you've got? We'll just wait here. You go and get some reinforcements." God is that confident in His ability. He can do anything He wants.

laughter on the battlefield

When everything seems stacked against us, and our situation seems the most hopeless, God is at His best. He becomes almost mischievous in the way He plans to deliver us. We see this several times in Scripture and most clearly in the life of Gideon.

In Judges 7, Gideon had gathered 32,000 men to fight the evil Midianites. Outnumbered four to one, we can all imagine Gideon's thoughts at that instant: *If everybody fights to the best of his ability, we might just have a chance.* His lieutenants were probably walking through the troops, rallying them. "Each of you just has to kill four guys and then you can have a coffee. Kill four—go to Starbucks" (my own paraphrase).

Meanwhile, in heaven, God had a mischievous look on His face. "Don't you think Gideon's got too many men there?" He said to an angel. "I mean, this may not be fun. And besides, I know these guys. If by some fluke they get a victory, they'll be obnoxious to live with for the next forty years. They'll break their arms patting themselves on the back." So, God decided to lengthen the odds in the enemy's favor:

"The people who are with you are too many for Me to
give the Midianites into their hands, lest Israel claim
glory for itself against Me, saying, 'My own hand has
saved me.' Now therefore, proclaim in the hearing of
the people, saying, 'Whoever is fearful and afraid, let
him turn and depart at once from Mount Gilead.' "

Judges 7:2-3

Gideon's lieutenants must have choked at that
announcement. Suddenly, the only thing they could
smell was burning rubber in the parking lot, as 22,000
men went home, leaving the Israelites outnumbered
sixteen to one.

But God in His merriment had not finished, as we
read in Judges 7:4-7:

But the LORD said to Gideon, "The people are still too
many; bring them down to the water, and I will test
them for you there. Then it will be, that of whom I say
to you, 'This one shall go with you,' the same shall go
with you; and of whomever I say to you, 'This one shall
not go with you,' the same shall not go." So he brought
the people down to the water. And the LORD said to
Gideon, "Everyone who laps from the water with his
tongue, as a dog laps, you shall set apart by himself;
likewise everyone who gets down on his knees to
drink." And the number of those who lapped, putting
their hand to their mouth, was three hundred men; but
all the rest of the people got down on their knees to

drink water. Then the LORD said to Gideon, "By the three hundred men who lapped I will save you, and deliver the Midianites into your hand. Let all the other people go, every man to his place."

Gideon was left with just three hundred men, less than one percent of what he started with. "Now surround the enemy," God ordered, leaving Gideon even more confused. *I couldn't have surrounded them with 32,000*, Gideon probably thought. *How am I going to surround them with three hundred?*

That night, God again spoke to Gideon.

"Do you want a prophecy?" He asked.

"Yes, please," Gideon replied.

"Okay," God said with a broad grin on His face. "Go down to the enemy camp and I'll give you one there."

Can't I have one here? Gideon probably thought.

Only God would send a man to the enemy's camp for a prophetic word. He is the only One confident enough to come up with that kind of plan. Gideon tiptoed through the camp of more than 100,000 enemy soldiers and somehow found himself outside the tent of the one man who was having a crazy dream, as we read in Judges 7:12–14:

Now the Midianites and Amalekites, all the people of the East, were lying in the valley as numerous as locusts; and their camels were without number, as the sand by

the seashore in multitude. And when Gideon had come,
there was a man telling a dream to his companion. He
said, "I have had a dream: To my surprise, a loaf of
barley bread tumbled into the camp of Midian; it came
to a tent and struck it so that it fell and overturned, and
the tent collapsed." Then his companion answered and
said, "This is nothing else but the sword of Gideon the
son of Joash, a man of Israel! Into his hand God has
delivered Midian and the whole camp."

Again, Gideon was stunned. *Loaf–sword. Loaf–
sword. I don't get it,* he probably thought. But the
enemy was prophesying their own destruction—and
that was more than enough for Gideon to trust
anything God asked him to do.

The next day, Gideon had his three
hundred men lined up and ready.
Following another bizarre command of
God, he collected every man's shield,
replacing it with a pitcher.

> "Happiness is a thing to be
> practiced, like the violin."
> John Lubbock

"Just do what I do," Gideon said.
"But I need my shield," a soldier no doubt replied.
Then Gideon handed them all a trumpet.
"But I don't play the trumpet!" another soldier said.
God had a deliberate, incredible, miraculous plan for
the Israelites' battle against Midian. With God, it's not
about the way we fight; it's about His mischievous,
happy nature.

the promised land

Years before, God had employed another odd strategy on another Israelite battlefield. The nation had just crossed the Jordan River into the Promised Land. Their new leader, Joshua, had been given a brilliant divide-and-conquer strategy for taking the land that God had promised them generations before.

I like to imagine some of the individual stories those Israelites saw unfold. For example, imagine Simeon and Rachel, as newlyweds, crossing the river into the Promised Land. *What a great honeymoon!* they thought. Everything around them was new and wonderful. They were just setting up camp when the horn blew for another men's meeting. A quick smooch—"Awww, our first kiss in the Promised Land"—and off Simeon went to meet with the other men.

Simeon walked down the road to the meeting place. Rachel, meanwhile, fussed over camp, setting up the cooking area, the bed and the rest of their possessions.

The men arrived at the gathering, and Joshua stood up, his hand hidden behind his back.

"Guys, I have a word of the Lord for you," he said.

"Cool," someone yelled out. "Our first prophecy in the Promised Land!"

Joshua brought his arm from behind his back. In his hand was a flint knife. "Thus saith the Lord," Joshua said. "Drop your trousers." (Or words to that effect.)

As murmurs rippled through the meeting, Joshua spoke about circumcision and a sign of the nation's covenant with God. Everyone had their hands crossed in front of them and asked, "Why now?"

It would have made more sense for God to have done this during the forty years they wandered in the wilderness. After all, how were these men going to fight and conquer the mighty city of Jericho when they would be walking like John Wayne for three weeks?

Meanwhile, back in her tent, Rachel had her best dress on, her hair done up and a delicious meal cooking. She kept looking up the road, thinking, *Hmmm, long men's meeting.*

In the men's meeting, the most astute of the Israelites realized that while Joshua had a knife, he had no sharpening stone. They deduced that it would be best to get this over with quickly, before the blade dulled.

Rachel's supper was now overcooked. She was angry, and she began yapping with her neighbor—her mother—about what was taking those men so long. After a few more hours, she saw some guys walking down the road very, very slowly.

What's taking them so long? she wondered.

Simeon walked through the tent flap.

"What took so long?" his young bride demanded. "Why are you walking funny?"

"Don't ask," he replied.

God is so supremely confident in who He is that He will lengthen the odds of His victory. In a Promised Land full of giants and powerful kings and armies, God ordered his warriors to be circumcised. God rendered His army completely incapable of fighting because He knew what He was doing. He wanted to be the Israelites' provision and protection. God laughs at His enemy.

contrition and joy

David knew that to fully know God, he had to embrace the joy God experiences every day. In Psalm 51, David wept and repented for his sinful actions with Bathsheba. He was completely remorseful for what he had done: "Create in me a clean heart, O God, and renew a steadfast spirit within me," he prayed in verses ten and eleven. "Do not cast me away from Your presence, and do not take Your Holy Spirit from me." But look at what he prayed next: "Restore to me the joy of Your salvation, and uphold me by Your generous Spirit" (verse 12).

Joy and gladness are the currency on which heaven runs. In that psalm, David also prayed, "Make me hear joy and gladness, that the bones You have broken may rejoice" (verse 8). Our joy is removed when we sin, but it's one of the first things God restores when we repent. He gives us that internal ability to smile and be happy no matter what is happening around us. Joy is deep-rooted happiness in the presence, person and nature of God. It sits in our heart and directs our life, displacing grief, mourning and sadness. When we have a quiet, God-given joy bubbling up inside us, the negative is pushed out.

> "Happiness is the only good. The time to be happy is now. The place to be happy is here. The way to be happy is to make others so."
>
> Robert G. Ingersoll

Beholding and becoming joyful doesn't detract from the difficulty of our situation—but joy actually helps us cry better. "Those who sow in tears shall reap in joy," Psalm 126:5 says. When God's joy is continuously present, we are not worn down by things. We are buoyed by who God is, and have developed an internal disposition to smile and be cheerful.

This joy enables patience to do a deep work in us. It's the cheerfulness of God that sustains us. Think about this: It is impossible not to smile when someone near you is laughing with all their might. An outrageous laugh is irresistibly contagious.

not enough laughter

There is simply not enough laughter on the earth right now. We need more contagious merriment. What if part of our role as ambassadors of the Kingdom of heaven is to bring laughter, joy and gladness back into our communities? What if we are called to spread the sheer happiness of being involved with the happiest Person who has ever lived? Laughter and joy are contagious and can be caught from someone else. We are designed in a way that allows us to catch the joy of the Father and spread it to others.

> "We cannot really love anybody with whom we never laugh."
> Agnes Repplier

"A merry heart does good, like medicine, but a broken spirit dries the bones," says Proverbs 17:22. Laughing with God heals our hearts. "The light of the eyes rejoices the heart, and a good report makes the bones healthy," says Proverbs 15:30.

People sometimes ask me, "How can I be joyful when all of this bad stuff is happening?" But the real question to ask is, "How can I not be joyful when I am connected to the one Person who can change everything, and who is, Himself, amazingly happy?"

For people who don't know God, life may be hard, even hopeless. Continuous joy and happiness are elusive unless you know the Author of all joy. There is no reason for us to be miserable.

A difference exists between happiness and joy. Happiness depends on something happening, but joy depends on knowing the One who is eternally happy. God is always taking great joy in making things happen. He delivered impossible victories to both Gideon and Joshua, and loved every moment of it. Today, God wants to restore the merry joy and cheerfulness of our salvation. He welcomes the possibility of being served by people with joyful faces. God wants His people to obtain joy, especially in the toughest times and worst circumstances.

Isaiah 35 is a beautiful prophecy about this part of God's nature. In the wilderness, He bursts forth in joy. "The wilderness and the wasteland shall be glad for them, and the desert shall rejoice and blossom as the rose," Isaiah 35:1–2 says. "It shall blossom abundantly and rejoice, even with joy and singing." In the land of the weak, the feeble, the brokenhearted and the lost, joy will spring forth, God promises. "And the ransomed of the LORD shall return, and come to Zion with singing, with everlasting joy on their heads. They shall obtain joy and gladness, and sorrow and sighing shall flee away" (Isaiah 35:10).

Joy is not an after-death experience; it is something we are called to develop today. It is a lifestyle promise. God has an incredible ability to keep joy at the center of our being. He is eternally happy, and that happiness is therefore part of our own being. We cannot avoid joy because it is part of the anointing of Jesus.

In Luke 4, Jesus walked into a synagogue and read out His prophetic mission statement, found in Isaiah 61. Look at the anointing He carried:

> The Spirit of the Lord GOD is upon Me,
> Because the LORD has anointed Me
> To preach good tidings to the poor;

He has sent Me to heal the brokenhearted,
To proclaim liberty to the captives,
And the opening of the prison to those who are bound;
To proclaim the acceptable year of the LORD,
And the day of vengeance of our God;
To comfort all who mourn,
To console those who mourn in Zion,
To give them beauty for ashes,
The oil of joy for mourning,
The garment of praise for the spirit of heaviness;
That they may be called trees of righteousness,
The planting of the LORD, that He may be glorified.

Isaiah 61:1–3

Jesus' gift of oil of joy for mourning is not a symbolic act—it is a real-life experience. He always turns our mourning into dancing; we cannot avoid joy. In this great prophetic confirmation of the life of Jesus, we begin to understand the purpose of the Father in Christ. He seeks to take our sadness and mourning and replace it with comfort, a garland of praise and the oil of joy. That was and is a rich part of the anointing on Jesus. His people are marked with blessing and laughter.

acquainted with grief

The Holy Spirit is extremely committed to sharing God's joy with us. In times of sadness, sorrow and grief, He is our great Comforter, seeking to return joy to us. That's His job and His passion. He doesn't pat us on the head or give us trite answers; He indwells us. *Let's get through this together,* He says. *We need to let joy bubble up again.* At times, sorrow is a necessary emotion, but we cannot allow it to take root in our heart. If grief fills our soul, there is no room for the Spirit to come in. While grief is meant to be a temporary emotion, joy is a permanent one.

In Isaiah 53:3, Jesus was prophesied as "a Man of sorrows and acquainted with grief." Note the term *acquainted.* He didn't live in grief, despite the crushing weight He carried. He was only acquainted with it. Verses 4 and 5 go even farther:

> Surely He has borne our griefs
> And carried our sorrows;
> Yet we esteemed Him stricken,
> Smitten by God, and afflicted.
> But He was wounded for our transgressions,
> He was bruised for our iniquities;
> The chastisement for our peace was upon Him,
> And by His stripes we are healed.

Jesus suffered these things so that we could be saved. This grief frees us from living a life of sadness and despair. These awful emotions can now only touch us temporarily. God rejoices over us, every day, with singing. His heart is glad when He looks at us because

Jesus opened the way for happiness, joy and cheerfulness to be permanent fixtures in our lives. The sacrifice of Jesus robbed us of the power to be miserable.

"Blessed are you who weep now, for you shall laugh," Jesus said in Luke 6:21. He has given us true, deep, real joy, and it is now a spiritual act on our part to choose to laugh with Him. We must tune into the happy heart of God and be like Him. "All the days of the afflicted are evil, but he who is of a merry heart has a continual feast," says Proverbs 15:15. Hearing the laughter of God brings out the best in us.

> "Laughter is the tonic, the relief, the surcease for pain."
> Charlie Chaplin

The Holy Spirit is more than our Comforter, however. He is also our Teacher and Friend. He loves to show us His ways and nature. When He connects with us, He smiles broadly. And when we connect with Him, we cannot help but grin back. He is irrepressibly happy in everything He does.

thriving in life

Heaven thrives on joy and gladness. When those two elements combine, there is a double portion of joy, laughter and cheerfulness. Gladness is the outrageous, external manifestation of a deep-rooted internal permission to be happy. God has given each of us the

permission to laugh, smile and be happy—especially
when everything in life seems stacked against us!

Joy doesn't even up the score with things that cause
us grief; it actually puts us in the lead: "Jesus, the
author and finisher of our faith, who
for the joy that was set before Him
endured the cross, despising the shame,
and has sat down at the right hand of
the throne of God" (Hebrews 12:2).

> "I am persuaded that every
> time a man smiles, but much
> more so when he laughs,
> it adds something to this
> fragment of life."
> Laurence Sterne

Paul was astonished by the
Macedonian church's ability to capture
the joyful nature of God. In 2 Corinthians 8:1–7, he
held them up as an example to the church in Corinth:

> Moreover, brethren, we make known to you the grace
> of God bestowed on the churches of Macedonia: that in
> a great trial of affliction the abundance of their joy and
> their deep poverty abounded in the riches of their
> liberality. For I bear witness that according to their
> ability, yes, and beyond their ability, they were freely
> willing, imploring us with much urgency that we would
> receive the gift and the fellowship of the ministering to
> the saints. And not only as we had hoped, but they first
> gave themselves to the Lord, and then to us by the will
> of God. So we urged Titus, that as he had begun, so he
> would also complete this grace in you as well. But as
> you abound in everything—in faith, in speech, in
> knowledge, in all diligence, and in your love for us—
> see that you abound in this grace also.

We are called to this same thriving quality of life, that no matter our circumstances, we live in the promise of God's joy. It is impossible to keep God from being happy, and because of that, His Church cannot be denied joy either. Sadness and grief can only overlay our joy; it cannot prevent a breakthrough into it. We may have to look hard on days for that cheerfulness, but it is always present in the heart of God. Sadness must be infiltrated by joy.

Abraham's wife, Sarah, had tried for decades to have a baby. At ninety years old, she had given up, even though God had promised her and Abraham a son and heir. In Genesis 21, God remembered that pledge, and the couple became pregnant. At age one hundred, Abraham was changing diapers at 3 A.M. God did the impossible, and Sarah's reaction was pure joy: "God has made me laugh, and all who hear will laugh with me" (verse 6).

Sorrow can lead us down a path to unbelief but joy will always take us into faith, as 1 Peter 1:6–9 teaches us:

> In this you greatly rejoice, though now for a little while, if need be, you have been grieved by various trials, that the genuineness of your faith, being much more precious than gold that perishes, though it is tested by fire, may be found to praise, honor, and glory at the revelation of Jesus Christ, whom having not seen you

love. Though now you do not see Him, yet believing,
you rejoice with joy inexpressible and full of glory,
receiving the end of your faith—the salvation of your
souls.

Becoming like Jesus leaves us with "joy inexpressible."
All we can do is laugh.

conclusion

Being joyful is not an option for the children of God. It
is the only true witness to a life that is eternally happy
and continuously cheerful. We have to become like
God is in all things, and that includes a sunny
disposition. Heaven is full of laughter. Everyone there
laughs and smiles, because they are in the presence of
God.

Heaven is a place of exuberance, and we must bring
that enthusiasm to earth. All of heaven—the Father, the
Son, the Holy Spirit, the angels, the saints—they all
love to rejoice. Everything that God makes and touches
manifests His happiness. It is embedded into our DNA.

"The kingdom of God is not eating and drinking, but
righteousness and peace and joy in the Holy Spirit,"
Paul wrote in Romans 14:17. "But the fruit of the Spirit
is love, joy, peace ... " he added in Galatians 5:22.

We must laugh, just as God laughs. No matter what
the circumstances, we have the physical, mental,

spiritual, emotional and legal power to rejoice as heaven rejoices.

Joy is a shield against doubt and unbelief. *"Ask, and you will receive, that your joy may be full,"* Jesus implored (John 16:24). When we pray, we should be bursting with joy at what God is about to do. We have the awesome privilege to receive joy from Jesus Himself.

Beholding and becoming throws all "measurements" out the window. The Father doesn't want to give us a "measure" of anything. His only scale is infinite. He wants us to be like Him, and He doesn't *measure* love and joy—He *is* love and joy. God wants all of us to be full of love, full of joy, full of laughter and full of gladness. He wants His qualities to fill us so full that they run off on to everyone around us. With Him, we can have everything we ever dreamed of—and far more.

A Prayer

Father,
    I pray that I will love You with
    All my heart today,
    That my mind will dwell in worship
    On You,
    That my will and emotion (or lack of it) will bend towards
      adoration
    Of Jesus,
    That my strength and energy of life will bless
    And glorify You,
    That every thought and word will give
    You pleasure,
    That every action of mine this day will make
    You smile.
Jesus deserves nothing less.
    In His name,
    Amen.

exercise 1:
lamentation

Lamentation is a powerful, and meaningful, form of
worship because it places our love for God above
even the worst circumstances in our life. No one in
Scripture models this form of worship better than
Job.

One day, Satan walked into heaven and had an
interesting conversation with God.

"Where have you been?" God asked.

"I've been roaming the earth," the enemy replied.

"Have you noticed Job?" God said proudly. "He is
blameless and upright and fears Me like no one else on
earth does."

"Of course he does," Satan answered. "You've given
him everything. Take it away, and he would curse You
to Your face."

"Try it," God said. "Take everything from him but
his health, and let's just see what happens."

God gave permission for a season, and the enemy

stripped Job of everything he could, even his children. Still, Job stood and blessed God's name.

Satan returned to heaven and upped the ante. God gave the enemy permission to take Job's health, and still the man stood. It was in the midst of this torment that we see the strength and depth of Job's love for God. "Though He slay me, yet I will trust Him," he lamented in Job 13:15.

Job stood fast, turning his agony into worship. He took everything we have been trained to fear: total disaster, complete ruin, hunger, disaster—even death—and praised the Lord.

God does not ask us to deny the existence of our suffering. He does want us to collect it, stand in those things and make Him an offering. The Holy Spirit, our Comforter, helps us to do this: He aligns Himself with our will and says, *I will help you to will to worship God.* The glory of the majesty of God is that He helps us *will* and *do.*

Too often, we either back away from our grief when we come to worship, or we quit worshiping at all in the face of the pain. We feel like we have to come to Him at our best, highest point. But God's heart is to accept us as we are. He wants us to step into that pain and worship Him with it.

The psalmists understood lamentation as well. In Psalm 42, the writer poured out his heart to God, laying out all of the difficulties he faced:

As the deer pants for the water brooks,
So pants my soul for You, O God.
My soul thirsts for God, for the living God.
When shall I come and appear before God?
My tears have been my food day and night,
While they continually say to me,
"Where is your God?"

When I remember these things,
I pour out my soul within me.
For I used to go with the multitude;
I went with them to the house of God,
With the voice of joy and praise,
With a multitude that kept a pilgrim feast.

Why are you cast down, O my soul?
And why are you disquieted within me?
Hope in God, for I shall yet praise Him
For the help of His countenance.

O my God, my soul is cast down within me;
Therefore I will remember You from the land of the
        Jordan,
And from the heights of Hermon,
From the Hill Mizar.
Deep calls unto deep at the noise of Your waterfalls;
All Your waves and billows have gone over me.

The LORD will command His lovingkindness in the
        daytime,
And in the night His song shall be with me—
A prayer to the God of my life.

I will say to God my Rock,
"Why have You forgotten me?
Why do I go mourning because of the oppression
    of the enemy?"
As with a breaking of my bones,
My enemies reproach me,
While they say to me all day long,
"Where is your God?"

Why are you cast down, O my soul?
And why are you disquieted within me?
Hope in God;
For I shall yet praise Him,
The help of my countenance and my God.

Lamentation does not deny the existence of pain; it does just the opposite, in fact. It actually involves worshiping God *with* that sorrow. What are the circumstances of your life? Are you in the winepress of God, being crushed like a grape? What is the sorrow you are feeling? If you have none, don't dig it up: Just be blessed, and live life to the fullest.

If you are in mourning, you have the opportunity to worship in the most powerful way possible: lamentation. This worship isn't done in order to have God remove the pain. It simply recognizes that God stands in the moment with us. Lamentation elevates God in the presence of our enemies. It brings out a side of God that other forms of worship simply cannot touch.

In this exercise, we will craft our own prayer of lamentation, focusing on two words: *though* and *yet*. Again, if you are not in a season of grief, rejoice and move on. But for those of you in a season of mourning, try this exercise.

1. Find a quiet place before God. Rest in His glory. Close your eyes. Ask Him to stir up the Holy Spirit He has deposited in you and to draw as near to you as possible.

2. Simply *be*. Just drink in His presence. If your mind begins to wander, bring it back to the wonder of God. Give yourself to Him completely.

3. Take a pen and write down the *though* circumstances in your life: the challenges you are currently facing, the pain you feel, the grief you haven't shared. Make an offering to God of the things that have wounded you.

   Though . . . .
   . . . .
   . . . .
   . . . .

   Though . . . .
   . . . .
   . . . .
   . . . .

Though . . . .
. . . .
. . . .
. . . .

Though . . . .
. . . .
. . . .
. . . .

Though . . . .
. . . .
. . . .
. . . .

4. Now rephrase your worship for God: *Though* these
   things have happened, *yet* what will you do? Don't
   ask Him for anything; simply bless and honor Him.
   Don't let anything stop you from exalting Him.
   Write your promises and worship to God in a series
   of *yet* statements:

   Yet . . . .
   . . . .
   . . . .
   . . . .

   Yet . . . .
   . . . .
   . . . .
   . . . .

Yet.....................................
....
....
....
Yet.....................................
....
....
....

Yet I will worship You.

5. Now go back and re-read your *though* and *yet* statements, as a psalm of lamentation to God. Use it to worship God in your quiet time with Him. Add and change verses as you deem necessary over the next several weeks and months.

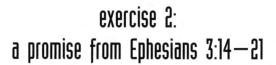

exercise 2:
a promise from Ephesians 3:14—21

Ephesians 3:14–21 carries an important piece of the
puzzle of simply resting in God and becoming more
like Him. Let's read the passage:

> For this reason I bow my knees to the Father of our
> Lord Jesus Christ, from whom the whole family in
> heaven and earth is named, that He would grant you,
> according to the riches of His glory, to be strengthened
> with might through His Spirit in the inner man, that
> Christ may dwell in your hearts through faith; that you,
> being rooted and grounded in love, may be able to
> comprehend with all the saints what is the width and
> length and depth and height – to know the love of
> Christ which passes knowledge; that you may be filled
> with all the fullness of God.
>
> Now to Him who is able to do exceedingly
> abundantly above all that we ask or think, according to
> the power that works in us, to Him be glory in the
> church by Christ Jesus to all generations, forever and
> ever. Amen.

To become rooted and grounded in love, we must immerse ourselves in the love of Christ every day. Jesus' love needs to be so real to us that our minds, our hearts, our heads, our speech, our hands become conduits of that love of God.

Learning to love as God loves breaks down the issues in our lives. Our poor self-image shifts as we see ourselves as Christ sees us. Our history falls by the wayside without a word of counseling or deliverance. God simply infects us completely. When a divine outpouring of the love of God comes, there is a displacement of the wounds we currently have.

The best thing we can do to prepare for such a revelation of God's love is to quickly get rid of any grudges and bitterness onto which we have been holding.

Take a few moments and pray. Ask God if there is anyone toward whom you hold ill will. Be sensible about this; we need to get rid of the things that are keeping us from the promise God has given us.

▶ List their names:

. . . .

. . . .

. . . .

▶ How can you restore those relationships? What steps do you need to take toward forgiveness? Choose to forgive, and ask God to bless those people.

Moola for Missions

...through April 23rd, there is a "Moola for Missions" can at Chick-Fil-A to put your receipts. 10% of all receipts will be donated towards our teens! If our youth group has the most receipts, we will get 20%!

Easter Eggstravaganza SOFT candy needed

Easter Eggstravaganza is coming Saturday, April 16th. Candy donations are needed from everyone (SOFT candy, please) - please drop off at the Children's Check-in booth or in the church office by THIS Wednesday, April 13th.

Church Membership

If you are interested in becoming a member of BedNaz, or just learning more about the Nazarene denomination, you are invited to a Church Membership class today at 12:30 pm. You can support our teens and bring your spaghetti dinner to Sherman Hall B!

▶   Write a prayer of forgiveness and blessing.

....
....
....
....
....

It may not be possible to see the relationship restored or reconciled. But if it is possible, then you need to go for it, expecting the grace, love and support of the Holy Spirit. If restoration is impossible, write a card with a blessing (do it anonymously, if it helps) and send it to him or her. Make the blessing substantial and significant.

Forgiveness clears the decks of resentment and opens our hearts to be baptized in God's love. If we do this, His promise to us is concrete: "You, being rooted and grounded in love, may be able to comprehend with all the saints what is the width and length and depth and height—to know the love of Christ which passes knowledge; that you may be filled with all the fullness of God." God is able to do far more than anything we can think to ask: "Eye has not seen, nor ear heard, nor have entered into the heart of man the things which God has prepared for those who love Him" (1 Corinthians 2:9). God's power of love wants to work in you and redeem the time that has been wasted.

The Holy Spirit is calling all of us to learn to live in the outrageous goodness of the majesty of the love of

God. He wants us to move in such love that no one is safe from receiving a blessing from God—on the streets, in the coffee shops, on the highways and byways. The love that we carry, birthed out of a Mary-like, restful, intimate relationship with Jesus, can change any situation in a heartbeat.

God wants us to fully engage with Him in this season, because He intends to fully engage with us. It is a time to be wholehearted in our affection for God, becoming the son or daughter we were always meant to be.

exercise 3:
Lectio Divina

Lectio Divina (Latin for "divine reading") is an ancient way of reading the Bible—allowing a quiet and contemplative way of coming to God's Word. *Lectio Divina* opens the pulse of the Scriptures, helping readers dig far deeper into the Word than normally happens in a quick glance-over.

In this exercise, we will look at a portion of Scripture and use a modified *Lectio Divina* technique to engage with it. This technique can be used on any passage of Scripture; I highly recommend using it for key Bible passages that the Lord has highlighted for you, and for anything you think might be an "inheritance word" for your life (see my book *Crafted Prayer* for more on inheritance words).

> God is our refuge and strength,
> A very present help in trouble.
> Therefore we will not fear,

Even though the earth be removed,
And though the mountains be carried into the midst
of the sea;
Though its waters roar and be troubled,
Though the mountains shake with its swelling.

Selah

There is a river whose streams shall make glad the
city of God,
The holy place of the tabernacle of the Most High.
God is in the midst of her, she shall not be moved;
God shall help her, just at the break of dawn.
The nations raged, the kingdoms were moved;
He uttered His voice, the earth melted.
The LORD of hosts is with us;
The God of Jacob is our refuge.

Selah

Come, behold the works of the LORD,
Who has made desolations in the earth.
He makes wars cease to the end of the earth;
He breaks the bow and cuts the spear in two;
He burns the chariot in the fire.

Be still, and know that I am God;
I will be exalted among the nations,
I will be exalted in the earth!

The LORD of hosts is with us;
The God of Jacob is our refuge.

Selah

1. Find a place of stillness before God. Embrace His peace. Calm your body, breathe slowly ... clear your mind of the distractions of life. Ask God to reveal His rest to you. Whisper the word, "*Stillness.*" This can take some time, but once you're in that place of rest, enjoy it. Worship God out of it.

2. Read the passage twice, slowly.

   a. Allow its words to become familiar to you and sink into your spirit. Picture the scene— become part of it. Listen for pieces that catch your attention.

   b. Following the reading, meditate upon what you have heard. What stands out? Write it down.

   . . . .
   . . . .
   . . . .
   . . . .
   . . . .

   c. If a word or phrase from the passage seems highlighted to you, write it down.

   . . . .
   . . . .
   . . . .
   . . . .
   . . . .

3. Read the passage twice, again.

   a. Like waves crashing onto a shore, let the words of the Scripture crash onto your spirit. What are you discerning? What are you hearing? What are you feeling? Write it down.

      . . . .
      . . . .
      . . . .
      . . . .

   b. What is the theme of this passage? Write it down.

      . . . .
      . . . .
      . . . .
      . . . .

   c. Does this passage rekindle any memories or experiences? Write them down.

      . . . .
      . . . .
      . . . .
      . . . .

   d. What is the Holy Spirit saying to you? Write it down.

      . . . .
      . . . .
      . . . .
      . . . .

4. Read the passage two final times.

   a. Meditate on it.

   b. Is there something God wants you to do with
      this passage? Is there something to which He is
      calling you? Write it down.

      . . . .
      . . . .
      . . . .
      . . . .

   c. Pray silently. Tell God the thoughts this
      Scripture is bringing to your mind. Ask Him
      for His thoughts. Write down your
      conversation—as if you and God were sitting
      in a coffee shop, two old and dear friends,
      sharing.

      . . . .
      . . . .
      . . . .
      . . . .

5. Pray and thank God for what He has shared with
   you. Come back to the passage a few more times
   over the coming weeks.

FAQs
(frequently asked questions)

Q. *Who is Graham Cooke and how can I find more information about him?*

A. Graham Cooke is a speaker and author who splits his time between Southampton, England, and Vacaville, California. He has been involved in prophetic ministry since 1974. He founded and directed the School of Prophecy, which has received international acclaim for its advanced series of in-depth training programs. Graham is a member of Community Church in Southampton (UK). He is married to Heather, and they have three children: Ben, Seth and Sophie. You can learn more about Graham at:

www.grahamcooke.com

or by writing him at:

P.O. Box 91
Southampton
England SO15 57E.

Q. *How can I become a prayer partner with Graham?*

A. Check his website, www.grahamcooke.com, for all of the information you need.

Q. *Has Graham written any other books?*

A. Graham has written several other books: *A Divine Confrontation: Birth Pangs of the New Church* (Destiny Image), *Developing Your Prophetic Gifting* (Chosen), *Crafted Prayer* (Chosen), *God Revealed* (Chosen), *The Language of Love* (Chosen), *The Secret of a Powerful Inner Life* (Chosen) and *When the Lights Go Out* (Chosen). All are available at most Christian bookstores or at www.grahamcooke.com.

about the author

Graham Cooke is married to Heather, and they have three adult children: Ben, Seth and Sophie. Graham and Heather divide their time between Southampton, England, and Vacaville, California.

Graham is a member of Community Church in Southampton (UK), responsible for the prophetic and training program, and working with team leader Billy Kennedy. In California, he is part of the pastoral leadership team, working with senior pastor David Crone. He has responsibility for Insight, a training program within the church and for the region.

Graham is a popular conference speaker and is well known for his training programs on the prophetic, spiritual warfare, intimacy with God, leadership and spirituality. He functions as a consultant, specifically helping churches make the transition from one dimension of calling to a higher level of vision and ministry. He has a passion to build prototype churches that can fully reach our postmodern society.

A strong part of Graham's ministry is in producing finances and resources to help the poor, supporting many projects around the world. He also financially supports and helps to underwrite church planting, leadership development, evangelism and health and rescue projects in the third world. If you wish to become a financial partner for the sake of missions, please contact Graham's office, where his personal assistant, Carole Shiers, will be able to assist you.

Graham has many prayer partners who play a significant part in his ministry. For more information, check his website.

Contact details for Graham Cooke:

► **United States:**
Vaca Valley Christian Life Center
6391 Leisure Town Road
Vacaville, CA 95687

email: fti.admin@vvclc.org

► **United Kingdom:**
Sword of Fire Ministries
P.O. Box 1, Southampton SO16 7WJ

email: admin@swordfire.org.uk

► **Canada:**
Jenny Bateman,
Friends at Langley Vineyard
5708 Glover Road, Langley, BC V3A 4H8

email: jenn@shopvineyard.com

► website: www.grahamcooke.com